FALL

poems by

Diane Vreuls

Finishing Line Press
Georgetown, Kentucky

FALL

Copyright © 2020 by Diane Vreuls
ISBN 978-1-64662-333-4 First Edition
All rights reserved under International and Pan-American Copyright Conventions. No part of this book may be reproduced in any manner whatsoever without written permission from the publisher, except in the case of brief quotations embodied in critical articles and reviews.

ACKNOWLEDGMENTS

Thanks to Martha, who asked for a haiku.

Publisher: Leah Huete de Maines

Editor: Christen Kincaid

Cover Art: Sarah Friebert

Author Photo: Diane Vreuls

Cover Design: Diane Vreuls

Order online: www.finishinglinepress.com
also available on amazon.com

Author inquiries and mail orders:
Finishing Line Press
P. O. Box 1626
Georgetown, Kentucky 40324
U. S. A.

*

The first red leaf

Sets fire to the hedges

Leaves fall like ash

*

*

Raking leaves

Reaper rhythm

Harvest of hill

*

*

Seeds and hunger

Meet at our feeder

The cardinal cries

*

*

Ants heading hillward

Cross over our driveway

With pennyweight loaves

*

*

Secret villagers

Share our address:

Rabbits, voles

*

*

The skirmish at the birdfeeder?

Unrecorded

By Herodotus

*

*

Wind wakes

Scrubs clouds, combs pastures

Chases itself, and gone

*

*

Stone's breath

Trees' tattered hymnal

Treble sky

*

*

Moon in the window

Taking a selfie

(The glass laughs)

*

*

Overhead travelers

Jet through the darkness

Swifter, my dreams

*

*

Deer bunk free

In our woodlot

B&B

*

*

Slow

Starshift

Fast day

*

*

The earth drains of color

The finch, the oak

But ah, the sunset

*

*

First frost

Brittles grass

Berms, bones

*

*

Snow falling

Tolling

Time

*

*

As the past is more than we remember

Today is not the future

We dreamt

*

*

Siren song

They say it's the all-clear

We say it's the warning

*

*

Can't we do

A system restore

Of the universe?

*

*

We blame our way out of the Garden

When what we need to do

Is plant

*

*

Faith

Is the door

That keeps blowing open

*

* * *

Diane Vreuls was born in Chicago and took a B.A. from the University of Wisconsin and an M.A. from St. Hilda's College, Oxford, where she was a Marshall Scholar. Her work has appeared in *Best American Short Stories, Commonweal, The Paris Review, The New Yorker* and elsewhere. She has published a novel, *Are We There Yet?*, a collection of short stories, *Let Us Know*, a children's book, *Sums*, and two books of poetry, *Instructions* and *After Eden*. A new collection of poetry, *Windrift*, will appear from Black Mountain Press in 2021.

www.ingramcontent.com/pod-product-compliance
Lightning Source LLC
LaVergne TN
LVHW041525070426
835507LV00013B/1827